The Hopper

Written by Liz Miles

Illustrated by Rupert van Wyk

Collins

Nan has a hopper.

We hop off for food.

We zoom higher for butter.

We get eggs at a farm.

7

We get jam at a fair.

We hop on a boat for shellfish.

Nan cooks eggs with leeks.

The hopper

🐾 Review: After reading 🐾

Use your assessment from hearing the children read to choose any GPCs, words or tricky words that need additional practice.

Read 1: Decoding

- Look at the word **food** on page 3. Ask the children to segment it into its three letter sounds (phonemes) f/oo/d. Point to /oo/ and practise the sound, then ask them to sound talk and blend the sounds together.
- Do the same with the following words:

  higher h/igh/er   farm   f/ar/m   hear   h/ear   boat   b/oa/t

Read 2: Prosody

- Model reading each page with expression to the children. After you have read each page, ask the children to have a go at reading with expression.
- On pages 14 and 15 show the children how to use the story map to retell the story of the hopper's journey in their own words.

Read 3: Comprehension

- Turn to pages 14 and 15 and recap the different places Nan and the child visited on the hopper.
- For every question ask the children how they know the answer. Ask:
  o What did the characters in the book go out on the hopper to get? (*food*)
  o Can you remember some of the places they went? (*mountains, farm, fair, boat*)
  o Look at page 5. Why do you think the child asked Nan to zoom up? (*because a goat was ramming the hopper*)
  o Where would you like to bounce to on a hopper?